Crate Training for Puppies

How to Crate Train Your Puppy Easily in Just 3 Days! - Includes Tips Every Puppy Owner Needs to Know

Booker Brown

©Copyright 2021 – Andy Morrison - All rights reserved

The content contained within this book may not be reproduced, duplicated, or transmitted without direct written permission from the author or the publisher.

Under no circumstances will any blame or legal responsibility be held against the publisher, or author, for any damages, reparation, or monetary loss due to the information contained within this book, either directly or indirectly.

Legal Notice

This book is copyright protected. This book is only for personal use. You cannot amend, distribute, sell, use, quote, or paraphrase any part, or the content within this book, without the consent of the author-publisher.

Disclaimer Notice

Please note the information contained within this document is for educational and entertainment purposes only. All effort has been executed to present accurate, up-to-date, and reliable, complete information. No warranties of any kind are declared or implied. Readers acknowledge that the author is not engaging in the rendering of legal, financial, medical, or professional advice.

Table of Contents

Introduction 4

Chapter 1: Familiarizing your puppy to the crate 8

Chapter 2: The Advantages of Crate training 18

Chapter 3: Which is the best crate for your puppy? 24

Chapter 4: Fun Crate Activities 32

Chapter 5: Three-Day Crate Training Schedule 39

Chapter 6: Crate training at Night 45

Chapter 7: Housetraining your puppy 50

Chapter 8: Crate training problems 60

Chapter 9: Ameliorating Separation Anxiety with Crate training 72

Chapter 10: Mistakes to avoid when crate training 76

Chapter 11: TOP tips for crate training 83

Chapter 12: Puppy Crate training Q&A's 87

Conclusion 91

Introduction

Dog owners want a well-behaved dog who does not destroy stuff and goes outside to potty, and dog crate training plays a crucial part in having a well-trained dog. It provides a secure setting in which your dog can learn responsibility and independence. Dog crates are used within homes to restrict dogs or puppies to one location. This may come across as cruel at first, but it is simply to keep him contained at times. Dog crates should not be seen as a jail for your dog, which is a common misconception among novice dog owners. The purpose of the crate is to create a habitat, which is what dogs would have had in the wild. While many people associate crates with being confined, dogs are naturally house animals who prefer to stay in small, enclosed spaces. Just like any part of training, crate training requires time, patience, and energy, but in turn, it can give your dog a safe place to stay when you are not around. It also means that your house will remain as you left it before going to work, therefore fewer damages and one happy homeowner or landlord.

If you are like most people, correctly training your dog with a crate will be time well spent. Crate training takes time and dedication, but it is a tried-and-true method for training dogs who act poorly because they do not know any different. If you recently got a puppy or dog, you can use the crate to keep him out of the house until he learns all the ground rules. Before I proceed, I would like to state that for the purpose of this book, I shall use the pronoun "he" to refer to both male and female dogs. A crate is also a safe option when traveling with your dog in the car or visiting places where he is not allowed to run around freely. If you were wondering whether traveling will still be possible after getting a puppy, just know that crate training can facilitate this. If you properly train your dog to utilize the crate, he will regard it as his safe haven and will gladly spend time in it when necessary. When the world around your dog becomes too loud or overwhelming, crate training takes advantage of your dog's natural impulses to seek out a comfortable, calm, and safe space. It is also useful for keeping dogs from chewing on things around the house while housetraining. Because dogs do not like to litter their dens, the primary use of a crate is for housetraining. While they comprehend other rules, such as not chewing on furniture, the crate can limit access to the rest of the house. A crate is not a miracle cure for dog misbehavior. A dog can feel imprisoned and frustrated if the crate isn't used properly. This book will delve into the best crate for your dog, how to utilize it for travel, explore fun crate games, and how to train your dog to use the crate in just three days. This book teaches you how to go from not having a crate in the house to your dog enjoying spending time in it and even seeking it out as their favored resting spot on their own. It takes time to teach your dog that their crate is their personal unique happy area, a place where only nice things happen so that they are eager to spend peaceful, comfortable time there. A crate-trained dog will enter and exit their crate without being forced, would be fine being locked in sometimes, and will be peaceful within, making no fuss and displaying no signs of stress. If you try to confine your puppy without first going through a crate training process, they will almost surely be terrified, isolated, and fear the crate instead of loving it.

If your next concern is how long this training process can take, rest assured that your puppy can be crate trained in as little as three days. So, there is no need to make arrangements to take a lot of time off work. While it is possible to crate train your puppy in just three days, some dogs may require more time to complete the training. If your puppy takes a few weeks instead of a few days, do not get discouraged. By taking tiny, gradual steps, such as gradually exposing your puppy to the crate and slowly increasing the time they spend in it, they will grow to appreciate it, and you will both benefit from the numerous advantages it provides. This book shall cover different fun activities you can start doing to familiarize your puppy with the crate. There are plenty of benefits of crate training your puppy, and these shall be discussed. Crate training may not be a plain sailing process as puppies may start whining, barking, or littering their crate, but do not worry; ways to overcome these hurdles shall also be discussed. Separation anxiety is a very common issue in dogs. Puppies may experience this when their owner seems to leave them to run errands, go out without them, or go to work. The crate can be used to control this behavior and reassure your puppy that you will return to them, but in the interim, they can find comfort in their safe space, the crate. Crate training may not be the ultimate solution for separation anxiety, and a professional may sometimes be required to intervene. If you intend to take your dog on domestic flights to travel, starting crate training early can yield later benefits.

There are many errors one can make while crate training their dog, and this book shall outline them to make sure you avoid making them. Depending on your dog's age, temperament, and previous experiences, crate training can take days or weeks. It is critical to remember two things with crate training: The crate should be connected to something pleasurable at all times, and training should be done in gradual stages. Do not go too quickly. This process will teach your dog responsibility and reduce their anxiety when you are not around and teach you how to be patient along the way. From the top tips of crate training to the major no no's, this book shall be the ultimate guide for your crate training journey, making it possible in just three days!

Chapter 1:
Familiarizing your puppy to the crate

The more dogs identify their crates with a comfortable state of mind, the more they will like spending time in it. If you put your dog in the crate while they are playing, they will want to come out and play some more. If you bring them in when they are calm, they will probably see it as a safe refuge. Begin by bringing them in for ten minutes at a time and gradually increase the time. To create a comfortable environment, some people use dog beds or towels, although this is not always the greatest option. Again, it is a case of experimenting. It is all dependant on the breed of dog you have; he may tear the dog bed apart or pee on it. The same thing can happen to chew toys if left haphazardly in their crate. They can sleep on the crate mat itself, which is not a bad thing. Dogs generally prefer hard surfaces.

Your dog will need to go out of the crate to play, eat, and relieve itself. Dogs do not want to soil their sleeping quarters, but if they go too long without going for a stroll, they may do so. The crate should not be regarded as a punishing environment for the dog. To get rid of this mindset, you can incorporate the crate in entertaining games where they can freely enter and exit the open crate until they learn it is a safe space to be in.

When you feel like your dog is ready, gradually increase the amount of time it spends inside the crate. It is not suggested that you spend six hours at a restaurant at once. Perhaps you should go have a cup of coffee and then return after an hour or so. I suggest you use a recording device to see what your dog is up to while you are gone. You may keep an eye on them whilst in their crate to see if they are relaxed or agitated. You can then make up for the time you were away when you return. People frequently wonder if they may keep food or water in the crate or if they can put a piece of their clothes in there to calm their puppy. They may also be wondering about where to keep your dog's crate in your house. Naturally, each dog and crate scenario is unique. In many respects, little puppies vary from adult dogs! Similarly, a puppy just starting crate training is in a different scenario than a dog who has become accustomed to and loves its crate. The location of your dog's crate is determined by the amount of space available in your house as well as your and your dog's preferences. As they move from sleeping adjacent to their owner to sleeping alone in a box, young puppies perform better when their crate is closer to their owner. Dogs are outgoing animals who can become distressed if they are left alone, leading to behavioral problems. If you are crate training, you can start in your bedroom if there is enough space. As they grow old, you can move their crate to a more convenient position in your house. It will also help you during the first several weeks of nocturnal potty training to have them close while they sleep in their crate. There is one drawback: if your puppy is a light sleeper and their sleep time is before you go to bed, the sounds or lighting in the room may interrupt their sleep and make it hard for them to fall back asleep if they wake up.

Overall, find a crate setting where your dog feels most at ease and can rest calmly, as well as where there is enough space. Try to choose low-traffic areas like by the couch in the living room or next to your desk if you work from home. If you chose the laundry room, make sure it is away from appliances, vents, or cords. Some dog owners may choose to station their crate under the stairs or under the island in their kitchen. Try to avoid locations in direct sunlight or close by a fireplace. Try avoiding areas like close to doors that are used frequently or lead to the outside. If you have indoor plants, try avoiding placing the crate next to one of these plants. Besides risking losing your plant, it may also be poisonous to your dog if he decides to chew on it.

In general, crate add-ons are ideal for providing your dog with a comfortable place to relax and sleep in their crate. What that item is, however, will be determined by your dog, their chewing habits, and potty-training progress. Some dogs like less cushioning, while others prefer to burrow in a nest made of their bedding. Whatever you put in, if anything, should ideally be both chew-proof and watertight. Another useful property to consider is that it should be easy to clean. Chew-proofing is not as necessary for mature dogs as it is for puppies, and waterproofing is not as important either. You do not have to worry about chew-proofing your senior dog's crate bedding, but the waterproof feature may become increasingly vital as they age and become elderly dogs. Orthopedic support bedding can assist relieve sore joints for older dogs.

Your fragrance could be soothing to your dog. Whether you should leave one of your t-shirts or another item of clothing in your dog's crate, however, is highly dependent on your dog. If they are going to chew it up, that is a no. It is not worth the money and worry of the operation they will have to have to get the item of clothes removed from their inside if they procced to swallow a piece of your clothing. Yes, leaving one of your shirts in the crate can be a fantastic way to leave a little part of you behind when you cannot be there yourself if they are not inclined to chew and eat it. The smell of your clothes can be very soothing for your dog while you are away because dogs have a very sensitive sense of smell.

You may have heard that leaving water in your dog's crate is a bad idea. This is mainly attributable to the risk of water bowls tipping over and creating a wet mess in the crate. However, with some fantastic clip-on water bowls and bottles for crates, leaving water in your dog's crate is encouraged. Or you can acquaint them with the lickable water bottle. Once you've shown them how to use a lickable water bottle the first time, they will be hooked. If your dog is still having difficulties with it, try smearing a little peanut butter or coconut oil on the drinking nozzle to encourage them to lick it. They will notice that as they lick, water comes out with it. It may take a few attempts, but many dogs eventually learn to do it. Water is a vital resource, which means your dog requires it to live because dogs easily get dehydrated. Dogs should have constant access to fresh water if it does not interrupt their toilet routines. If your puppy keeps accidentally peeing in its crate, especially at night, talk to your vet about cutting down their water supply an hour or two before sleep and throughout the night. They may also want to rule out medical issues like urinary tract infections as a cause of frequent bathroom accidents. Some medical disorders, such as diabetes insipidus, diabetes mellitus, kidney condition, Addison's disease, or if they are on medical treatment that makes them more prone to dehydration, require a dog to always have unrestricted access to fresh drinking water.

Feed their meals in their crate while leaving the door open if you want your dog to like having their meals in the crate. Use a puzzle feeder to help your dog create positive relationships with their crate while also relieving boredom and providing enriching mental stimulation. Throw a few treats into your dog's crate for them to go retrieve whenever you are walking by their crate with your dog close behind. This will help them associate the crate with happiness! It is good to put some toys in your dog's crate while you are out unless you want them to be bored out of their minds and possibly become destructive as a result. Of course, not all toys are equal or made safe, and not every dog is ready for the privilege of having toys left unattended in their crate. The puzzle feeders are frequently your best bet when it comes to crate toys! Puzzle feeders, when chosen right, are often robust enough to withstand a little biting while remaining malleable enough to avoid fracturing your dog's teeth. These types of toys are great for engaging your dog and their brain when they are in the crate because they can be packed with food or treats. They do not have to be overly tough or overly filled, just enough to keep your dog occupied while you are gone.

You should keep lots of toys on hand for your dog. Toys that will allow them to release all their cooped energy, toys that will keep them occupied while you are gone, and toys that are just enjoyable for your dog. However, you must ensure that the toys are appropriate for your dog. It makes no difference how much energy it helps your dog burn off, how interesting it is, or how much excitement he has with it if a particular toy is harmful, unhealthy, or just plain bad for him. As with any toy, keep an eye on your dog when they play with it the first few times to check that they are playing correctly. Some dogs are old enough to have a couple of stuffed animals in their crate while you are gone, but not all are. There aren't any stuffed toys that would be good to have in their crate while you are gone if you have a serious chewer and destroyer. If you have a sniffer or nibbler, on the other hand, there may be a few stuffed toys that can provide them with the comfort and enjoyment they seek. In their crate, dogs should ideally not wear a collar. This is because dangling dog tags and even collars can get caught between crate bars, putting pets in danger of strangling.

- Crate training is a vital part of pet ownership, and for many dogs, but not all canines, covering your dog's crate at night is suggested. Some dogs may like the security of a darker, contained location, while others may become nervous in such an environment. Dogs are den creatures who enjoy the privacy of an isolated place; it is natural for them to seek out an enclosed, dark room when they are terrified or need to relax. Many dogs benefit from a crate cover, such as a blanket or crate-specific sheet, because it can help reduce anxiety and comfort dogs by reducing neural activity, minimizing excitement, and barking. When dogs are in a covered crate, they are less likely to respond to movement outside windows or in other parts of the building. A closed cover at night may signify that it is time to go to bed, while an open one may imply that it is all right to play. A covered crate might be especially useful on a road trip for a dog who is disturbed by long journeys or when put in unfamiliar environments. A gradual introduction, like crate training, is the ideal approach to get your best friend adjusted to a covered crate. Because a well-trained dog sees his crate as a secure and joyful place, you should never cover it with a blanket or cover to punish him. Instead, provide a covered crate as a place to relax. Cover the top of the crate with a blanket or fitted cover, tucking the draped material up to leave the sides exposed. Allow your dog to enter the partially covered crate on its own and gradually increase the amount of time he is expected to spend within, lower one side of the cover after a few days. Lower the material over a second side of the crate once your dog has accepted one side is covered. Allow the cover to hang over a third side after he has grown accustomed to two covered sides. For good behavior, provide lots of praise and treats. As with any part of dog training, consistency is crucial. To ensure that your dog is content and does not chew or rip the cover, do not leave him unattended until he has adjusted to a covered crate. Covering your dog's crate is very safe if you follow a few simple rules:

- Because it can obstruct airflow, you should never totally cover your dog's crate.
- Keep blankets away from heat sources,
- Make sure the fabric is breathable, and
- avoid snatch-up knit blankets.

In humid summer weather, keep an eye on the conditions inside the box to make sure it doesn't grow too hot. Puppies go through a chewing stage that is natural for them. Puppies may chew more than usual between the ages of four and eight months because they are teething, and they may shred bedding and any blankets or covers within reach.

It is claimed that covering the top, back, and sides, or only the top, can be more comforting for your dog. There will be fewer distractions, and the surroundings can be slightly darker, warmer, and quieter. It may be simpler for your puppy to rest and be peaceful when inside his crate if there is less stimulation. Secure the cover if your dog is prone to chewing. This will prevent him from pulling it into the crate and chewing or swallowing it. A dog cage cover should be made of a breathable, easy-to-clean material. An insulated cover may be advantageous if you live in a cold location or your dog spends most of his time outside, but it may be excessively warm otherwise. An appealing wire crate can be disguised with a specific crate cover that fits your decor. In a pinch, carefully tucked sheets or blankets will suffice if you take care not to create tripping risks for yourself or chewing or tearing dangers for your dog. To avoid overheating in the summer, consider proper airflow. Choose material that is easy to fit and remove for any size crate when making a fitted crate cover. If your dog is bothered by noise, consider covering his crate with moving blankets or furniture pads to decrease the amount of noise he is exposed to. Moving blankets have padding between layers of fabric to muffle unwanted noises such as domestic appliances, outdoor traffic, and, to a lesser extent, storms. Though a dog crate cannot be soundproofed entirely, absorbing blankets can be used when there is disturbing noise. When utilizing a crate cover, keep an eye out for signs of nervousness in your dog. A blanket over their crate may not be appreciated by all dogs; for others, it may induce more worry than relief. Some dogs will accept a crate that is only partially covered, while others will prefer a crate with no cover at all.

To summarize, if a covered crate is not helping your dog, leave it open. While not every dog enjoys the privacy of a covered crate, it might be beneficial to anxious or energetic dogs. Your dog may enjoy the opportunity to relax inside his own personal refuge if you correctly introduce a crate cover. With practice, your pet will learn that a covered crate signifies bedtime and provides a relaxing environment.

Adult dogs and pups can both be crate trained in the same way, though puppies may learn more quickly. You may discover that once you've picked and set up your dog's crate, they become are naturally curious and want to examine it right away. Make sure the door is held open so it doesn't shut them in. If your dog chooses to investigate, reward them. Knowing your dog will help you figure out what kind of treats they like the best. Some dogs respond well to tons of praise, others to a few foods, and still, others just want to play with you, so adjust the incentive to your dog's preferences while they are exploring the crate. Not all dogs will investigate right away, and some may be wary of the crate altogether. This shouldn't discourage you; all it means is that you will have to keep rewarding them when they choose to approach the crate. Move the food or toy to the door and then inside the crate as they build confidence. You can move to the next phase after they are confident going in and out of the crate on their own. Be consistent as much as possible if you want your dog to sleep in its crate at night. If you use a crate occasionally, your dog may become confused, and if they cannot foresee what will happen at night, they may become uneasy. They will be more relaxed if they stick to a routine because they will know what to expect.

From what to keep inside the crate to whether you should cover it or not, crate training is all about gradually familiarizing your puppy with his den-to-be. Always monitor your puppy in the crate to get a sense of what they enjoy and do not like, which can help you have an easy crate training experience.

Chapter 2:
The Advantages of Crate training

Although many dog owners feel bad about crate training their pets, confined areas provide a safe haven for dogs to rest and relax. Dogs, in fact, search for limited spaces to build protective helters for themselves. Crates are excellent training aids for pups, safe havens for elderly dogs, and lifesavers in the event of an emergency. Dogs that are secured during evacuations are less likely to become lost or injured. Crate training dogs from a young age is recommended by most veterinarians, trainers, and breeders. Because dogs do not like to ruin their sleeping quarters, crate training is an important element of housebreaking puppies. You will not have to clean up messes because they learn to hold their urination while in their crate.

Here are some of the benefits of crate training whether you have a puppy, an adopted senior dog, or a hunting dog:

- When you leave your dog home alone, you can rest assured that nothing will be soiled or destroyed and that he will be comfortable, safe, and not develop any negative habits.

- You can swiftly house train your dog by using the confinement to teach them control, establish a regular outdoor elimination schedule, and avoid accidents at night-time or when your dog is left unsupervised.

- When your dog is restless, over-excited, or bothered by too much noise or activity, you can successfully confine them.

- You may travel safely with your dog and be confident that he will adapt to unfamiliar circumstances more readily if he has his familiar comfort blanket and his crate.

- They can enjoy the peace and security of their own den, which they can retire to when they are tired, stressed, or sick.

- They can learn to control their bowels and associate moving their bowels with the outdoors more easily, so it will help with potty training too.

- When they need to be prohibited from some things, they will not have to suffer the loneliness and frustration of being isolated from their family in the basement or outside.

- Instead of being left alone on family activities and trips, they can take part even if they are in their crate.

- Crate training is an excellent technique to teach your dog to expect and appreciate alone time while also conditioning relaxed behavior. Your dog will come to cherish the time spent in the crate once he has been properly taught.

- When you cannot watch over your dog personally, a crate is a fantastic way to keep them from getting into danger. If you are busy cooking, working from home, or doing anything else that requires your full concentration, it is the ideal time for your dog to relax in its crate.

- A crate protects your dog from potentially harmful substances. A crate might be a valuable tool if your dog enjoys chewing on stuff. If a dog, especially a puppy, is left to his own devices without supervision, he may consume anything dangerous or toxic.

- Crate training is useful for dogs who need a break from a busy household or a familiar location to rest in everyday life. Crates assist dogs in learning to self-soothe or deal with their discomfort in stressful situations such as fireworks, thunderstorms, or renovation works.

- It also aids dogs in successfully confronting unfamiliar situations, such as having people over for family events.

- Crates make long-distance travel or vacations with your dog safer by allowing you to carry your dog safely by car or by air. Long vehicle rides are enjoyable for both humans and dogs when they are crate trained. Crates allow dogs to lie down and sleep while the driver focuses.

- Because dogs must be contained on flights, knowing how to behave in a crate during a flight is very crucial. This will help you avoid sedating your dog during flights because sedation may cause heart or respiratory issues in some breeds, according to some veterinary associations.

- Early crate training reduces the introduction of unwanted stress later in a dog's life. Older dogs do not need the added stress of learning new rules while coping with ailments like incontinence, arthritis, or animal neurological problems.

- Crate training helps elderly dogs with health concerns by providing a relaxing environment in which they can rest their joints or take frequent naps, prevent overnight wandering, and make transportation to vet appointments easier. Crates provide a safe haven for senior dogs as well. When surrounded by hyperactive children or other dogs, they may be especially in need of this.

- A crate offers the luxury of not having to struggle for their own place for rescue dogs. Because some rescue dogs are afraid of people, crates provide safety. This is the case for dogs who have experienced neglect or abuse in the past. Crates provide rescue dogs the assurance that they have their own space and that no one can hurt them.

- Many rescue dogs do not have socialization skills, which can lead to destructive behavior or excessive barking. Crate training will boost their self-esteem and help them stop misbehaving. If barking or whining becomes a problem during crate training, there are ways to deal with this, and it shall be discussed later in the book.

- Crate training is beneficial to hunting dogs since it keeps them comfortable during hunts and while traveling. Hunters will appreciate being able to contain wet and filthy hounds, so this is a win-win situation.

Crate training for travel

Purchase your dog's travel crate as soon as you know you will be moving or need to travel with your dog. This will necessitate some research and measurements to ensure you get the right one. Pets are in a much better position to enjoy a low-stress move or travel if they have a few weeks to become used to their crate. If your dog has never used a travel crate before and you suspect they will be wary, do not assemble it right away; instead, set the bottom half in your living room or similar common area where your dog spends time. Add the top of the crate once they have gotten comfortable with it. When your dog is completely at ease, you can go ahead and install the door and start using it fully assembled.

Though crate acclimatization is critical, do not rush the process. If you have some time, do let your dog accept the crate as a positive or at the very least neutral part of life, try to act as though nothing has changed during that time, and allow your dog time to adapt to the change of environment on its own. When your dog is used to the crate, keep them in it with the door closed while you run some errands. After this has gone well, you can try getting the dog and crate into the car and taking brief rides around town to show the dog that crate life isn't such a bad thing. Food, positive reinforcement, and compassion go a long way in encouraging new habits, and working on this goal together will deepen your bond and ease tension as you prepare for your big move. Traveling with a pet necessitates crate training. The pet must be transported in a travel-compliant crate while moving internationally. Your pet's comfort on an overseas journey is primarily determined by how comfortable they are in the crate. Taking your pet on a drive is the easiest way to imitate flight conditions. If your pet appears to be in distress, be sure to encourage and reassure them. It is beneficial to bring goodies with you on the trip. Some airlines will not accept a sedated pet, besides, sedating dogs on an airline in high altitudes may have its repercussions, so although your vet may provide such a solution, it is always best to have your dog crate-trained to avoid issues during travel.

The benefits of crate training do not lay only in the protection it offers to the owner's household but also in the peace it offers to the dog. Understanding the benefits of crate training can be as important as the first steps taken to introduce your dog to the crate. If used properly, the crate can provide peace of mind, security, and stress-free life, to both the dog and the owner, as I've previously stated.

Chapter 3:
Which is the best crate for your puppy?

By now, you probably know the benefits of crate training and have figured out a spot to put your crate around the house but are still torn between the different types of crates and which one is the best for your dog. There are various types of crates, and the choice is dependent on many different factors like the size of your dog, where you intend to use it, whether you wish to travel with it, and the breed of your dog, amongst others. There are various dog crates available, including soft crates, plastic and wooden, metal crates, large and small, foldable and non-foldable, heavy-duty or incredibly mobile, airline-approved crates, and travel-friendly crates, and more. With so many options, deciding on the ideal type of crate for your dogs can be tough. I shall explain all these different criteria, including the different types of crates, so you are able to make an informed decision before getting your first crate.

Types of Crates
1. Soft-sided crates

The walls of soft-sided dog crates are composed of soft mesh material or something similar. Some soft crates include a steel tube structure that makes the crate look more like a cage or den, while others resemble a rucksack or carrying case. Crates with soft sides are most popular among pet owners. Soft-sided dog crates are fairly priced, light, and easy to carry around, and dogs usually enjoy them as well. Soft dog crates are not the greatest alternative for every dog or every circumstance. Airplane and vehicle travel is best suited for soft-sided dog crates. They are ideal for travel because of their portability. This type of pet crate has been certified for usage in many airlines' cabins. They are particularly portable due to their small weight. Soft pet crates can be folded and put away in storage. These are also the comfiest crates for your pet. Soft-sided dog crates aren't ideal for dogs who have the habit of chewing on stuff, scratching, or get anxious while they are confined. These pet crates do not last very long and aren't very robust. They are the most difficult to clean. This means they are not suitable for dogs who haven't been trained to use a crate or go potty yet. As a result, most dog owners opt for these crates when traveling by car, airline, or other modes of transportation. Always use a seat belt to keep your dog in his cage and ensure that the crate does not slide or move around in the car.

2. Plastic Crates

Plastic crates are a good compromise between soft-sided and metal dog crates. They are not the most attractive crates on the market; in fact, most of them seem cheap and unappealing; yet, depending on why you are buying one, it might just do the job, and it comes with its own set of benefits. A plastic dog crate is more durable than a soft-sided box and will provide your dog with a bit more privacy than a metal wire crate. However, even with all the holes in the crate, the ventilation is not always adequate, and the dog cannot stay in there for lengthy periods of time. Depending on the type of plastic box you buy, it may or may not be easy to clean. With plastic crates, a quick hose washing could suffice. They are long-lasting. It is difficult to break the thick plastic. When not in use, they can be stacked on top of one another. Because they are enclosed and thick, they give the dog the feeling of being in a "home." Because their sight is limited, they can assist in keeping energetic dogs calm and quiet. Most airlines have given their approval for in-cabin and below-seat use of these plastic crates. Because plastic crates do not fold flat, they are more difficult to store. They are sturdy, but because they are made of plastic, some dogs may be tempted to chew on them. Plastic absorbs smells, so even though they are easy to clean, they can develop a persistent dog stench after a while.

3. Metal Crates

When people think of crates, they usually think of metal dog crates or big crates. These crates are precisely what you'd expect: a metal-wire construction that is well-ventilated and gives you and your dog plenty of visibility. Metal pet crates are the ideal alternative for puppies who chew a lot because it is practically hard for the crate to be destroyed, but some larger dogs can manage to do so. The best features are their durability, visibility, and increased airflow, but the biggest disadvantage is that they are heavy and tough to transport. Heavy, robust cages constructed of tougher metal are available for large and strong dogs; they are frequently more expensive and not travel-friendly, but they are impossible to damage. Fortunately, many metal crates are designed to fold readily for rapid dismantling, allowing owners to take them with them wherever they go. They are also simple to keep clean. Some even feature removable bottom trays for easy cleaning. This cage does not absorb scents and will remain odorless. These crates are ideal for dogs who enjoy being involved in all family activities since the crates provide a complete view. These pet cages will rust over time because they are constructed of metal. Because this is a heavy sort of crate, even if it folds up, it can be difficult to move due to its weight.

4. Wooden Crates

As the name implies, most wooden dog crates place a premium on fashion and style. They typically match your home decor and are the most attractive of all the pet cages discussed in this chapter. Many pet owners who know that their crates will not be moved frequently or that they will be used as stationary cages while also having travel options will choose a wooden dog crate and keep it in one location at home for their dogs to relax. While wooden dog dens are the most attractive and may even add to the style décor of your home by serving as a nightstand or a table, they are also the heaviest, difficult to clean, and not all dogs react positively to them. Even though wooden decorated crates retain all the features of other types of crates, they lack flexibility, adaptability, and ease of use of plastic, metal, or soft-sided pet crates. There aren't many good-looking decorative dog crates made of wood to pick from. They are not suitable for dogs who enjoy destroying furniture. These containers can be ruined by chewing and clawing. Because they are made of wood, they are difficult to clean and remove odors. When compared to other types of crates, these crates are on the pricey side.

5. Combination crates

Combination crates are exactly what the name suggests: a mix of the crates listed above. Combination crates can be the greatest sort of crate for dogs in some situations, but only in a few. They are composed of a mix of metal and plastic crates. The bottom has wheels to make transportation easier. They feature doors that are easy to open and close. They are usually very heavy. These cages are extremely difficult to construct and will most likely require the assistance of numerous people.

6. **Exercise pens**

Exercise pens, or Ex-pens for short, are another sort of puppy and dog confinement system. Ex-pens, unlike crates, have an open top and are more adaptable in terms of shape and size, as you can often modify the shape and size to meet your space as well as your dog's size and maturity level.

How to choose the best crate?

These and other considerations will influence your decision on the finest type of crate for your pet. A soft-sided dog crate, for example, will not fit if your dog enjoys chewing and is an aggressive chewer. Alternatively, if you plan to utilize the crate for travel, a heavy wooden crate is not the best option. For choosing the best crate for your dog, start by asking yourself the following questions:

- What will you do with your pet crate?
- What exactly do you and your dog need it for?
- Are you going to take it with you on your trip?
- What is your dog's personality like?
- Is it necessary for the dog crate to match your home's decor?
- What is the maximum amount you are willing to spend?

- <u>Is it necessary for the crate to be easily transported because you will be moving it frequently?</u>

The breed is also an important factor to take into consideration when buying a crate for them. It is suggested to measure your dog before hunting down the perfect crate. This is how you should measure your dog:

- Measure your dog from the nose tip to the base of their tail while they are standing on all fours. Do not include their entire tail length in this measurement, as this will result in a kennel that is too big. For the optimal crate length for your dog, add two to four inches to this measurement.

- Take their measurement from the floor to the tip of your dog's head while they are sitting. For the minimum height suggested for your dog's crate, add two to four inches to this dimension.

- You will not need to measure the width of the dog crate because it'll be determined by the length and height measurements.

- If you will be carrying the crate around with your dog inside, double-check that your dog is under the manufacturer's suggested weight limit for the crate you purchase.

Buying an adult-sized cage and adjusting it to accommodate your puppy is a good way to save money. This way, your puppy may grow into the crate. A divider is included in most wire or metal crate models, allowing your puppy to grow with the box.

Choose a dog crate that allows your dog to stand, turn around, stretch out, and lie down when determining how big it should be. Any extra space will encourage your pet to sleep on one side of the crate while relieving itself on the other. Many crates come with recommended weight ranges, but you should consider your dog's physical qualities as well as their weight. Consider the height and width of the crates while you shop to choose the most comfortable for your pet. A size chart is provided below to assist you in determining the size of your crate based on the size of your dog's breed:

- 18-22 inches — Extra Small Dogs
- 24 inches —Small Dog Breeds
- 30 inches —Medium Dog Breeds
- 36 inches — Large Dog Breeds
- 42 inches —Extra Large Dog Breeds
- 46 -72 inches— XXL Giant Dog Breeds

Make the crate pleasant and comfy once you've decided on the ideal size crate for your dog. Decorate the crate with a nice blanket, a warm bed, or a soft crate pad and place it in your living room. In addition to crate cover for increased protection, your dog will love having a new toy in his crate.

Containment is beneficial regardless of your pet's age. Wire crates, soft crates, plastic crates, and even furniture-style — with such variety on the market, it is crucial to know which one is best for your dog's training. In conclusion, the ideal type of crate to utilize to train your dog is determined by your lifestyle and goals and your dog's size and habits.

Chapter 4:
Fun Crate Activities

Crate games are entertaining for both pups and adults, and they serve to reinforce the skills learned via crate training. They also understand that when they are in the crate, pleasant things happen. Crate games also teach dogs impulse control, allowing them to stay focused even when there are several temptations. A dog with good impulse control understands that listening to its owner is more important than chasing other dogs or rushing down the beach. Even though crate games are essentially training sessions, the dog finds them to be a lot of fun. Your joy and enthusiasm will encourage the dog to keep doing the same behaviors it knows will make you pleased and provide it with a reward. Bring a bunch of high-value snacks with you, such as sausage pieces and cookies, and use them as rewards to praise excellent behavior frequently.

Try the following crate games with your dog:

1. **Where is the toy?**

Sit with the dog next to the crate and bring a chew toy so that the puppy can see what's going on. Put the toy in the back of the crate and shut the door after it is delighted about it. Standing outside, the dog will ideally begin to show signs of wanting to go fetch its toy, such as staring at you or pawing at the door. When the puppy is particularly enthusiastic, open the door and let it in on its own. Repeat this many times over a few days, and if the puppy appears to be relaxed, shut the door behind it and watch as it contentedly takes a seat and chews its toy.

2. Look here!

Once the dog has learned to sit in the back of the crate, make sure it is aware that you are holding one of its favorite treats, and then have someone else pass by the crate or throw a ball in front of it. If the dog remains seated with his gaze is fixed on you, open the door and lavish praise on it. Repeat this process several times before doing it with the door open. The goal of the game is for the dog to remain focused on you since the value in your hand outweighs the attraction of the other distractions around it.

3. In and out.

Begin by placing the dog in the crate. If the dog remains seated in the crate, open the door, and give it a treat. Step back from the crate and call the dog, who will run out to see you, but if you do not reward it, it will return to the crate, then you may quickly reward it with a tasty treat even if it doesn't sit. Repeat this process numerous times, each time going a bit further away from the crate. Because it is so happy, the dog will probably jump around you a few times when it first gets out, but it can only be praised once it has returned to its crate.

4. Advanced In and Out.

This game is like the previous one, but it has been enhanced by the addition of a tug toy. Hold the dog's tug toy behind your back and open the latch with the other hand once the dog is inside the crate. Only open the door if the dog is at the back of the crate. Show the toy to the dog and call it out, then play a brief game of tugging for a few seconds before removing the item and waiting for the dog to return to the crate. When it does, shower it with praise and goodies right away while keeping the toy hidden. Even with the toy distracting it, the dog should be able to return to its crate.

5. A game of fetch.

Set the crate with the door fully open, then stand a few meters away from the dog. Choose the dog's favorite fetching toy and spend a few minutes playing with it. Then toss the toy energetically into the crate for the dog to retrieve. If the dog is hesitant to enter, throw it near the door, then a bit further in until the dog can no longer resist. Increase the difficulty by moving away from the crate and hurling the toy straight in through the door with full strength. However, it may be required to cover the crate so that the toy does not fall out the back. Reward them with a treat when he returns the toy to you. If you have other dogs who know this game, line them up with their own crates so they may all play simultaneously. Even in the confines of a backyard, this game may be evolved into a highly fast-paced activity that will give the dog a terrific workout.

6. Modified game of fetch.

Play the same game as before, except this time, place the crate on one end and the swinging bed on the other. Begin by having the dog sit on the bed, then commanding him to run to the crate to retrieve a toy. As the dog's performance improves, increase the distance. The bed provides a satisfying conclusion to this game and aids in the development of the dog's skills for the next crate game.

7. Obstacle race.

Build various hurdles to increase the challenge once the dog understands that the goal is to get to the crate, retrieve a toy and return it to the swinging bed. Begin by constructing a tunnel and sending the dog from the hammock bed to the crate to retrieve a toy, which he will then bring back through the tunnel and onto the bed. If you do not have a tunnel, create one out of a line of chairs with the dog going between the legs. Other challenges could include winding around cones or jumping over items. The possibilities are unlimited once the dog understands the game and understands that there will be rewards at the end.

8. The crate is full of surprises!

This is a simple game. Place a few treats in your dog's crate when they aren't in the room, such as a favorite toy, hot dogs, or other snacks. Allow your dog to find the rewards on his own. The crate is not frightening; it is the bearer of delicious entertainment! The first few times you do this, leave the door open. Close the door for a few seconds while your dog is happily munching, then open it to let him exit if he appears comfortable and secure in the crate.

9. Tossing treats.

You can progress to more interactive games after your puppy is able to enter the crate on his own. Prepare a huge number of little cookies and start by throwing one into the crate. Make sure the dog can hear the treats landing in the crate. Leave your dog to enter the crate on its own, rather than urging or forcing it in. When the dog enters, praise them, call them back to you after they finish their treats, and then throw another into the kennel so they re-enter. Repeat for another five to ten minutes. Maintain a positive attitude and pay attention to your dog; if they become bored with the game, take a break; you can always play again eventually.

10.   Toss and close.

It is time to up the game by closing the door for short periods of time after your dog has gotten used to fetching treats thrown into the crate. Begin by putting a cookie into the mix. He'll come in to get the cookie, so close the door for a couple of seconds. The idea is for your dog to remain calm and quiet; if you close the door for too long, they will bark, whine, or scratch at it. If you open the door after they do any of these things, you are supporting their bad behavior. So, keep it brief and gradually increase the length of each training session.

11. Meals in the crate.

Simply said, your dog's meals should be fed in the crate. Start with the door open, but after a few days, you will discover that the dog is so enthusiastic about food that they will not notice if you close it. If you close the door, make sure to unlock it before they complete their meal so they can go out easily.

12. No rushing!

Our goal is for our dog to leave their crate in a nice and tranquil manner. This is for two reasons: first, a dog that bolts from its box may run into you or another person, and second, for safety. Assume you are taking your crated dog to the vet for a regular examination. When you unlock the car door and then the dog's crate, the dog runs from the crate into a crowded parking lot or into the road. Your dog must remain in one place unless you instruct it otherwise. You can educate a dog to leave calmly once they are familiar with being crated with the door closed. When your dog tries to run, the simplest method is simply closing the door and tossing a treat into the crate. Close the door when your dog comes in. Now go ahead and open the door. Praise your dog and give him a goodie if he stays put. Close the door if they start moving forward. Wait until he has regained his composure before opening the door a few inches. Close it if he moves forward. If he stays put, gradually open the door wider until you can give him a treat. Then, either call him out of the box or assign a release word like "ok," "release," or any other phrase you use to let your dog out of other instructions. The use of release words makes training a lot easier! Repeat this every five to ten minutes. It will not take him long to grasp that rushing out of the crate is not a good idea.

13. Creating a safe space.

You can start praising relaxation if your dog is comfortable entering the crate and shutting the door for some time. Remember, one of our aims is to make the crate a relaxing, tranquil environment for the dog. Give your dog a reward and tell them to lie down in their crate. Reward and treat. Do not let the dog out of their crate. Sighing, rolling onto its side, stretching, yawning, licking their lips, resting their head on their paws, and even blinking are all signs that the dog is calm. When they do one of these things, reward them with a calm "good" or "yes" or light petting. Avoid using large goodies or excessive praise. You may give them their release word when they have relaxed, and you have complimented them.

If the dog makes a mistake, never penalize it; this will simply draw attention to it and disrupt the tone of the training session. Rather, ignore the errors and spend some time figuring out where you went wrong during training. Before introducing new skills, reinforce the skills taught in the prior session at the start of each one. Then, at the end of it, both you and your dog will feel accomplished and likely have a greater connection than when you started.

Chapter 5:
Three-Day Crate Training Schedule

When you establish a schedule for your puppy, it learns to anticipate what will happen next, which helps lessen anxiety. Humans are the same way. When you know what's going to happen next, almost everyone feels better. A puppy crate training program is beneficial since it provides you with a set of daily actions to follow. If done correctly, a crate-trained dog can be trained in about three days. Keep in mind that puppies will go potty after eating, playing, and napping. You will note that a puppy cage training timetable follows a set of guidelines. Fifteen to twenty minutes of play, thirty minutes of feeding, and one to two hours in the crate is the standard schedule to begin with. Stick to the schedule but utilize your common sense as well. If you believe your puppy requires more playtime, go ahead, and give it to him. Take your dog outside right away if you suspect he needs to go potty. Two-month-old puppies can usually hold it for two to three hours, while an hour is added with every month they grow. From six months and beyond, they are usually capable of holding it for six to eight hours.

Crate confinement for significant amounts of time during the day should not be demanded of young puppies. Their small bladders make this challenging, and it will take time for them to form positive associations with their crate. Remember that each dog is unique. Some dogs may require more practice before staying in their crate for long periods, while others may fall in love with it immediately! The housebreaking process is sped up by structuring your puppy's days around a somewhat regular yet flexible pattern. This is because it helps you figure out when he must urinate or poop by regulating their biological clock and bodily processes. Meal times should be at the same time every day whenever possible. You do not need to bring a stopwatch with you or clock it down to the minute but aim for a variation of thirty to forty-five minutes. A consistent daily regimen not only benefits your dog physiologically but also helps him feel confident in his new surroundings and boosts his self-confidence. Even something as simple as keeping to a normal schedule can help a nervous, lonely puppy relax a little.

Try following this schedule to successfully crate train your dog in just three days:

At 7 AM, take your dog out for potty first thing in the morning as you both wake up. This should last about 15 Minutes. Right after he has done his business, spend time outside and play. Never lock your dog in the crate when he is filled with energy. He is more likely to stay quiet in his crate if he has exhausted his energy levels. Playtime should last for about 20 Minutes. At around 7.35 AM, let your dog sit in his crate with the door open and have him have his first meal inside the crate while you supervise him. This should include food and water and last for about 30 Minutes. After his first meal, take him out for potty again. This will ensure you have fewer accidents in the crate. Make sure you give him enough time to empty his bladder and bowels. Now you can either play games with your dog whilst outside; otherwise, you can play fun games inside with the crate. This should last around 20 Minutes. At 8.40 AM, you should let your dog in the crate so he can rest and relax while you get ready to go to work, run errands, or work from home. The time spent in the crate will be solely dependant on the age of your dog. You can extend the time they spend there as they grow older. This also depends on how long they can stay put without relieving themselves while waiting for you to take them out. -Start off with one to two hours, and gradually increase. At 11 Am take your dog out for potty to avoid accidents in the crate. If you cannot take your dog out yourself, you can get a dog sitter, a family member, or a friend to do this for you, and don't forget to let them know the training schedule. Allow at least 15 Minutes for him to go potty. Spend some time to play with your puppy after they have been potty. At 11:30 AM, let the dog spend some more time in their crate until it is time for their next meal. Start off with one to two hours, and gradually increase the time he spends in the crate. At 2 PM, take your dog out for a potty break. While outside, spend some more time outside and use it to play with your dog for about 20 Minutes. At around 2.35 PM, go inside and serve your dog their next meal in the crate. Mealtime should last for about 25 Minutes. At 3 PM after feeding time, take your dog out for another potty break. After play time, go inside and play some more games, ideally using the crate; this way, they can get more treats and understand that being in the crate is not bad after all. It would be ideal if this lasted for about 30 Minutes. It is now time for your dog to spend some more time in the crate. 6 PM would probably be when you would be returning home from work, so it is best to take your dog out of the crate and take them out for a potty break for 15 Minutes as soon as you return home. Your dog is probably very happy to see you are back from work and would appreciate spending some quality time with you. Extend the time they spend outside and use it as play time. Because the first few days of crate training need to be consistent, although you will be at home and available to supervise them whilst outside the crate, it is suggested to still place the dog in the crate for them to get used to it even when you are around. You can opt to add an interactive feeder with some snacks during this time to keep them busy. At 9 PM, you may feed them their last meal of the day. This should be about two hours before they go to sleep to avoid accidents in the crate. At 9:15 AM, take them out for their last potty break of the day. Use this time to play with your dog so they can be tired before going in the crate for the night. At 10 PM, let your dog go inside their crate for the night. Allow your pet to sleep in the crate in your bedroom at night. Let your dog stay inside its crate for the night. Leave them to sleep in the crate in your bedroom at night. Let him know you are still there, even if he is locked up in the crate. This will provide him with a sense of security and teach him that nothing unpleasant will happen to him while he is in the crate. Ascertain that the puppy will be at ease in his crate. Provide him with a comfortable bed or pillow in which he can relax and sleep. Put his favorite chew toys in there for him to enjoy. If they sleep well, he will always feel wonderful and not grouchy when he wakes up. Do not forget to give him a treat or two while he is inside the crate. He will certainly return to his crate at night for another undisturbed sleep after the pleasurable and comfortable experiences he has had with it.-If your dog is still a puppy, you may need to set alarms for you to wake up and take them out for a potty break outside because they are not yet trained to hold it for the entire night. So, the duration of their night inside the crate can vary based on their age.

Perseverance is key here, so make sure to stick to the above schedule for a consecutive period of three days, and your dog will quickly get used to their crate. This is obviously dependant on your lifestyle and your dog, as the above table is a guideline and not a strict must. You will notice that a lot of playtimes are incorporated in this schedule, and this is to exhaust their energy, and it also gives you more opportunity to incorporate the many fun crate games as mentioned earlier. Strike a balance between outdoor and indoor playtimes. Before starting this three-day crate training program, make sure you have already introduced your dog to the crate and have included it in games as well. In this way, they will already be familiarized with it and understand that their crate is exciting and secure to be in. Eventually, when they grow older, the potty breaks will decrease, and their time in the crate unassisted will increase. You will be able to let them be in their crate alone without supervision.

Every dog will learn and advance through crate training at a different rate, just like any other sort of training. Consistency, patience, and a lot of positive reinforcement are the keys to success! If you stick to persistent positive training, you will soon have a dog who enjoys his crate, as well as a safer environment and less stress in your life. If a puppy was introduced to cages early in life, crate training should be completed within a few days. It may take longer if they are unfamiliar with containers. If a puppy or adult dog has had previous negative experiences in a crate, it may take considerably longer to erase the bad memories and help them see that space as a nice place to be. Do not leave them in the crate all day, no matter how old they are. Crates aren't a replacement for a dog sitter. A dog who spends the entire day and night in a crate may develop anxiety and frustration. If you think you will be away from home for a long period of time because of work or other commitments, consider hiring a sitter or dog walker or enrolling your dog in day-care so they can get the physical and mental activity they require every day.

Chapter 6:
Crate training at Night

You need time and effort to crate train a puppy. You will soon be receiving that much-needed sleep that you've been missing as your puppy grows accustomed to their own nightly 'bedroom.' Raising a dog can be stressful, and many puppy owners suffer from puppy blues. In some ways, having a puppy at home is similar to having a human baby. When you add in the frustration of attempting to get your puppy to sleep through the night in their crate, the situation becomes much more unpleasant! Even if your puppy is eating well and napping in their crate during the day, sleeping in their crate at night can feel a bit overwhelming.

To succeed in house training, young pups require a lot of rest, as they can get irritable if they are exhausted, as well as a lot of bathroom breaks. Your puppy is constantly learning new things. You do not want them to feel lonely and begin whining because he is distressed. Their entire world has altered dramatically; formerly, they slept in close quarters with their siblings, but now they sleep alone in a crate. They may feel more secure if their crate is in or near your bedroom. Placing a snuggling toy inside the crate can also help relax a puppy who is getting used to sleeping alone because it mimics the warmth and heartbeat of a sibling. On the other hand, if there is a lot of movement or activity in the room, your puppy's sleep may be disrupted. Put their crate in a quiet corner or a separate, less-used area. You can also put your puppy's crate near your bed at night, and with the help of a sound machine, lessen any noises that might disturb their sleep.

Young puppies should be taken outside to relieve themselves around ten minutes after drinking water. When they drink water immediately before bed, their little bladders are more likely to become full during the night, necessitating a toilet break. For overnight crating success, think about their dinnertime; feed your puppy its last meal three to four hours before bedtime. This will allow their bodies to digest the food fully so they can potty outside before retiring for the night. Remember to take advantage of that last-chance restroom break! Before going to bed, the last person in your house should take the puppy out for another little walk. Giving your dog time before bed to run around and burn energy with mental enhancing activities can be very beneficial and help them fall asleep better. High-energy hobbies like fetch or tug-of-war might induce overstimulation in certain puppies. Choose your physical activity routines carefully, and do not overdo them before going to bed. Going on a sniffing adventure with your puppy is a fantastic and low-impact way to burn some energy before bed, given they have received the required immunizations for exploring outdoors. For puppies, mental activity is just as vital as physical exercise, and giving them puzzles and interactive toys before nighttime can help them relax and unwind. Enrichment activities throughout the day provide an acceptable outlet for your puppy's natural inclinations and habits, such as chewing or digging. To support a comfortable night's sleep for your puppy, establish a night-time routine for him. This should involve a quiet entrance into the crate for sleep, time to chew on a suitable toy for unwinding, frequent pee breaks to ensure they are running on empty, and then a calm evening meal a few hours before bedtime. What is in and outside your puppy's crate can have an impact on his sleeping habits, overall health, and safety. A home diffuser, in addition to a snuggling toy or a sound machine, can be utilized to relax your pet. Some puppies prefer to sleep on cold surfaces, while others prefer to nest in a pile of blankets. This is frequently determined by the sort of coat they wear or the temperature in your home. If you notice that your puppy kicks the blanket out of the way most of the time, they might sleep better in their crate with less covering. When they're not in their box, pay attention to where they like to lay down and rest. If you are concerned about potty accidents in your puppy's crate throughout the night, consider investing in a waterproof or easy-to-clean mat. If your puppy is prone to chewing, consider a more durable crate mat or a raised cot that is less appealing to chew on. Night-time crate training is extremely beneficial to your puppy's overall housetraining. However, it is critical that your puppy has consistent possibilities to go to potty outside during the night. Around sixteen to twenty weeks of age, a complete night's sleep without a restroom break is common. Crate training aids in housebreaking because dogs do not want to ruin their sleeping quarters. The purpose of nocturnal potty breaks is to allow your puppy to use the restroom before the next morning when they have to go right away. Setting the alarm for regular overnight potty breaks will help you avoid cage accidents and being awakened up by your puppy barking. You may generally expect three hours between necessary potty breaks for a two-month-old puppy. It would take four hours for a three-month-old puppy. You should expect a maximum of seven hours from dogs approximately six months old. Even if they are physically capable of holding it longer, small puppies just getting started with house training should be given a potty break several times during the day. If your puppy wakes up at 1:00 a.m. wanting to go to the bathroom, set the alarm fifteen minutes before for a proactive potty break. Set your alarm for thirty minutes later after a few days to test if they can hold it longer while sleeping. You should see a natural rise in the amount of time they spend between night potty breaks as their bodies mature. When you take your dog out at night for a potty break, avoid engaging in any play or activity that would agitate them. Pick them up and take them outside yourself if you can, as this will prevent them from flexing their legs too much and fully waking up. If they do not go to the toilet in five minutes, you take them out, simply return them to their crate, and put them back to sleep. If this happens frequently, it is essential to increase the time between night-time toilet excursions. Keeping a headlamp, collar or harness, leash, and poop bags at the door to go outside in the middle of the night will save you a lot of trouble.

If your dog pees in the crate, do not penalize them for it. Keep calm, take them outside right away to see whether they still need to go, and then clean up the mess properly. While accidents during toilet training can be the consequence of something going wrong throughout the process, that can also be a sign of possible medical concern. If simple and consistent improvements in the potty-training procedure do not fix the problems, or if they occur frequently, it is time to consult your veterinarian to check if there's a medical concern. It could take a lot of patience to train your puppy to sleep in a crate at night, do not give up! When you are tight on sleep and the alarm goes off to take the puppy outdoors for a pee break, it can be difficult. It would be much worse to wake up in the middle of the night to a barking puppy with a crate accident. In the long run, your crate training practice, perseverance, and patience will pay off. After your puppy has been consistently house trained, you can explore allowing them to sleep outside of their crate or even in your bed!

Chapter 7:
Housetraining your puppy

It is difficult to house train a puppy, but no one enjoys cleaning up doggy accidents. Taking advantage of the dog's den instinct is the first step in housebreaking a puppy or an adult dog. When properly introduced as a happy and rewarding environment, a crate empowers your pet with its own safe refuge. House training can be done in various ways, some of which are more effective than others. It is critical to use a cage as part of your house-training process because it is incredibly efficient at speeding up the process and, without a doubt, makes it easier and cleaner!

Potty training

A crate isn't just a valuable tool for speeding up house training; it also keeps your puppy safe at home and while traveling, protects your things, prevents bad habits from forming, and gives a dog a space to call its own where it can get some peace and quiet. You want to praise and reward them for going to the bathroom at the location you've designated as their bathroom spot, which is normally outside, though the same rules apply inside as well. You must keep your puppy from relieving itself somewhere you do not want them to, which is frequently within the house. Every time you congratulate them for going in the right area, it motivates them to do it again. Every time you keep them from doing their business in the wrong place, you prevent them from developing negative behaviors. After that, the habit becomes a part of living, and your puppy is housetrained. However, every time a puppy gets away with doing their business somewhere they shouldn't, a chance to teach them to go where they should is lost. The simplest approach to house-training a puppy is to have their toilet in the same area every single time and never have them toilet at a different location. Although this is obviously unattainable, the closer you get to this ideal, the faster your puppy will learn. The usage of a crate is one technique to get as close to this ideal as possible. Crate training your puppy instills in them the idea that their crate is their den, triggering their natural need to keep it clean, especially by not urinating or pooping in it. After all, no dog wants to sleep or lay in his own filth. When you cannot oversee your puppy, you can take advantage of their natural instincts by putting them in their crate. They will not pee until you release them, at which point you can take them to their designated bathroom area. This provides you additional chances to praise them for "doing it" in the right spot. The bulk of bathroom accidents occur when you are unable to see them. However, if you put them in the crate at these times, they will stay in it until you release them. As a result, crating drastically reduces the number of opportunities for your puppy to have bathroom accidents.

When a puppy is young, it will simply relieve itself whenever the urge stricks. They have no idea how to control it, they cannot stop it, and it astounds them just as much as everyone else when it happens. As a puppy grows older and their bodies mature, they can begin to 'hold it' for a short period of time. But, because they've grown up only 'dumping' whenever and wherever they feel the desire, with most likely their breeder cleaning up after them, they have no idea that they can or should keep it. When you place them in the crate, and they feel the urge to go, they will try to hold it as much as they can to avoid dirtying their den.

This tells the puppy that if the desire strikes, he can hold it and not have to go potty right away. This can significantly affect how quickly your puppy learns to use the bathroom. Whining, circling, sniffing, barking, or scratching at the door if your puppy is confined are all indicators that they need to leave.

Before you put your dog in the crate, make sure they've recently gone to their toilet location to avoid any extremely counterproductive accidents. Fifteen to twenty minutes before a scheduled potty time, depending on their age and size, place them in the crate to ensure no accidents occur in your home. They will be ready to go when their planned time arrives. Take them to their potty location, praise and reward them if they use it, and then let them back into the crate until just before their next planned time. Repeat this process until they empty themselves in the proper location before letting them leave the crate. Remember that every time they toilet somewhere they shouldn't, it will set back your house-training. So, leaving them in the crate when you cannot give them your undivided attention is ideal. Only use a crate that is the right size, not too big, and not too small. Never keep a puppy in a kennel for longer than he or he can contain their bladder. If you do, your puppy will have no choice but to use the crate as a bathroom. Never cage a puppy or dog who has a history of doing so. Some dogs or pups, especially those that have been rescued and fostered, may have picked up negative tendencies from their previous owners. Before using the crate, you should spend more time teaching them not to pee in the house.

Never cage a dog who has a medical condition or is sick with diarrhea. When they're sick or have diarrhea, crating them interferes with their need to be clean, and you will be forcing them to sleep in their own mess since they cannot control their bowels due to a medical condition.

If you catch them doing something wrong, clap loudly to let them know they've done something wrong. After that, call them outdoors or gently take them by the collar. Praise them or offer them a tiny treat when they're done. If you find evidence but do not see the act, do not get enraged and yell at them. Puppies are not capable of making the connection between your rage and their mishap. They could require extra time to comprehend what they've done wrong. To avoid odors that can entice the puppy back to the same location, clean up with an enzymatic cleanser. When greeting people or displaying submissive behavior, some puppies urinate out of enthusiasm. It is better to ignore these dogs when you first arrive and then allow them to approach you once you've sat down. Do not punish them, as this will only exacerbate the problem. It is generally outgrown if you ignore it. If the habit persists six months after bringing your dog in, your veterinarian may prescribe medication to help solve the problem, and you may also want to consult a behavior therapist to ensure that your puppy's confidence is restored. Finally, take your dog for a little stroll when he finishes going potty outdoors, and do not put him back in his crate the moment he enters the house. If they must go back to their crate as soon as the fun ends, some pups will pretend to take longer at relieving themselves to stay outside in the fresh air and enjoy your company; for a little longer!

Do not let anyone convince you: no method of house training is simple or straightforward! Although I believe that house training with a crate is the most successful and time-saving option, you cannot just buy one, put your puppy in it, and expect them to never dirty your home. Time, patience, commitment, and work are still required.

Feeding your dog in the crate.
One motive for feeding your dog in the crate could be to create a cheerful environment. The crate can appear frightening and threatening at first, so feeding them their daily meals in it makes it much more enjoyable. They'll want to run into the box as soon as you fill their food bowl! If you need to leave, they will be more ready to enter the box and stay in it. If you have multiple dogs, feeding them in crates can help reduce hostility. It allows each dog his own space to eat, removing the fear that another dog would take it away, and there is no need to worry about fights erupting if you leave them alone. It provides them with a comfortable environment in which to eat slowly. Many dogs have issues with food aggressiveness in general. In the crate, they can dine in peace away from children and other people who could bother them. Petting a dog while it is eating is never a good idea. Rescued street dogs or malnourished ones are more likely to guard their food; thus, the crate keeps all potential predators at bay. Many dogs prefer to eat meals near their water bowl. If your dog drinks a lot of water after a meal, feeding them in their crate may not be the greatest option. It will soak the crate and make a bigger mess. Your dog's shelter is supposed to be a clean, comfortable place for them to unwind. If your dog is a grazer, keep their food in an accessible area rather than a crate. They must eat sufficiently throughout the day; thus, it should be in a location that they pass by frequently. Remember that this method works best in a household with only one dog. The crate may or may not be the best location to feed the dog, depending on the

breed. See what happens if you feed them inside the crate for a week. You can always return their feeding station to its previous location. No matter where they are fed, a satiated dog is a happy dog!

Choosing the right commands for your puppy
The words you use to instruct your dogs to accomplish something are known as dog training vocal commands. They're simple to train your dog and can come in handy when your hands are occupied, or your pet cannot see you. You may teach your dog verbal cues by rewarding a specific behavior. For example, you can say "settle" as soon as or even before your dog relaxes and then award him with a treat when he obeys. Hand signals can be translated into verbal commands if your dog responds well to them. The key to teaching a dog to understand human language is repetition. Both physical and verbal cues are understood by your dog. These are all useful when you are crate training your dog. Verbal commands for dog training can be given in any language. Because these are words that are said only when you are talking to them, it might sometimes help dogs grasp them better, so try choosing words that are not so common and used continuously in any conversation like "ok." Make sure commands are short and sharp so you quickly get their attention. Make sure you pick words you can remember to avoid confusing your dog. A dog is more likely to understand a brief, incisive vocal cue that stands out from the rest of your jumble of words! You may come up with strange or amusing words to use as orders, but it might take some practice to say them correctly. Make sure you reward them when they obey, whether intentionally or coincidentally, in the beginning. If you predict their behavior, make sure you say

the command before he does the thing he is expected to do, and in the process teaching him the command and rewarding him for it. Make sure you always reward after he obeys the command and not before. You will have to make this choice based on your dog's training objectives. If you want your crate training journey to succeed, be firm with yourself and use unusual terms. If all you wish for a well-behaved pet, choose words that come naturally to you, as your furry friend will pick up on both your words and your body language. He'll be able to figure out what you are talking about with time.

If you have recently adopted a puppy that already responds to hand signals and you want to teach him verbal cues, follow these steps:

1. First, state the verbal cue clearly.
2. Make the hand gesture that your dog is already familiar with right after that.
3. Your dog's response should be noted and rewarded.
4. Repeat these steps numerous times!
5. Now try using the verbal cue instead of the hand signal.
6. Reward if he answers!
7. If he ignores your vocal command, remain patient and repeat until you get a response.

If you wish to teach a new command to your dog, follow these steps:

1. <u>During a training session, your dog should be performing the behavior for you regularly. This will happen if you give the behavior a lot of positive reinforcement!</u>
2. <u>Before you can add a command, your pet must be awarded at random.</u>
3. <u>Say your command loudly and clearly.</u>
4. <u>The next response from your dog should be noted and rewarded.</u>
5. <u>These steps should be repeated multiple times!</u>
6. <u>Ignore it if he does the behavior without your command!</u>
7. <u>These steps should be repeated until your pet only responds when you command.</u>

Do not repeat the phrase more than once while teaching your furry best friend the meaning of a word using the outlined steps! Before you try again, be patient and give him a chance to obey. If necessary, mentally count to ten. If you tell your dog to sit, sit, sit! He'll just learn that sitting doesn't mean anything but sitting, sitting, sitting! They will only obey when you repeat the phrase ten times, which is the last thing you want. It is critical that your dog learns the fundamentals of obedience. A dog that listens to your commands is more likely to stay out of trouble. Having a well-behaved dog makes it easier for him to stay safe. If you let yours off the leash or if he bolts from the house immediately he sees an open door, it is critical that he returns when called. Dogs who are well-behaved are also good neighbors. You don't want yours to be overly enthusiastic in front of a toddler terrified of dogs or an elderly neighbor with shaky legs. If your puppy is less than three months old, you should begin with very mild training straight away.

Begin with toilet training and household ground rules, such as where he sleeps, where he should stay during your mealtimes, which rooms he is permitted to enter, and whether he is permitted to sit on the couch. A dog's attention span is long enough at the age of three or four months to begin learning simple commands. Training establishes your position as the leader and is another way of spending quality time. Get the tools you will need before you begin. Your vet can help you purchase the right training collar and leash for your dog, considering his or his size and weight. You will also need a supply of little snacks to carry in your pocket. It is a rare dog that isn't driven by a tasty treat. To prevent confusing the dog, repeat each instruction with the same short word and his name. Keep training sessions to a minimum. The attention span of a dog is limited. Train three to five times daily for the basic commands, with each session lasting no more than ten to fifteen minutes. Remember that your dog only wants to please you. Praise elicits a positive response, while punishment elicits a negative response.

For commands associated with the crate, choose a spoken cue, such as 'crate up,' 'in your crate,' or 'go to bed,' to instruct your puppy to enter the crate. Choose a separate command, such as 'free,' for when you want him to come out of his crate. Take a few goodies and put two or three of them in the crate in the morning. Say the command as they enter to retrieve them, but only once. Praise the puppy and give him another treat after he has entered. To let him know he can exit, say your release order.

After ten repetitions, take a five-minute rest and restart the exercise. Organize a second training session later that day, this time without goodies. Say the enter command when your dog is close by. If he goes inside, praise him and give him a treat. Say the release command right away, so he learns to associate it with getting out of the container. Repeat the command ten times, then take a short break. Continue with the remaining part of this step after a few hours. Start by repeating the preceding exercise a few times to ensure he recalls the vocal signals, then instructs him to enter the crate once more. Praise and treat him, then close the door slowly for eight to ten minutes. Offer him more snacks during this time. Say the release order and open the door after the eight to ten minutes are up. If he barks or whines, ignore him for a few seconds until he falls silent; once he is, give him a treat or award him through praise and let him go out. Perform the exercise as you did in previous training sessions. After your puppy has left the crate, do not even give him any treats. When he is inside, good things should happen!

Love and patience can turn an untrained puppy into an obedient and extremely responsive dog.

Chapter 8:
Crate training problems

A dog may refuse to enter the crate. In the crate, it may bark or relieve itself and litter the area. Before you confine him to the crate, make sure you give him plenty of attention. Play with him, cuddle him, feed him his meals or treats, and make sure he is gone outside to relieve himself. Bring him inside, encourage him to sleep peacefully with you while you read or watch TV, and then carry him to his crate and place him inside with a tiny amount of food or biscuits when he is settled. He should be all right if all his needs are addressed and he is relaxed. A stuffed toy, a worn but dry towel with your scent in it, or a hot water bottle with a cover or a towel are all things that give a dog some comfort. For the first time in their lives, puppies that have recently left their mother and siblings are alone, which can be frightening. When he is in the crate, he may start crying, start scratching the crate door, and cry some more. The location of the crate is crucial since it prevents the dog from feeling isolated. Place the crate in a location where the puppy can see and smell people during the day, but not in the middle of human activity, when family members are in and out of the house and active. Put the crate in a location where family members may talk to him, cuddle him, and take him out when they have time to watch him.

The crate should be near someone's bedroom at night, close enough for the puppy to hear the person breathing. You should never choose an isolated area from the rest of the apartment, such as the laundry room or the garage. He has a strong desire to be with his new family. Some dogs aren't fond of being confined. If a dog has been kept in a crate for an extended period, he may decide that enough is enough. When confined and separated from their owner, dogs with separation anxiety will fight to get out of the crate. Some dogs, on the other hand, appear to make it a personal mission to demolish any crate they are confined in. These dogs, unfortunately, can injure themselves; some may break their nails, wound their paws, or shatter their teeth. Crates may not be the greatest choice for these dogs when it comes to preventing housetraining accidents or undesirable behaviors in the house. Make an appointment with a local dog trainer for these pets so the problem can be diagnosed and a possible remedy administered.

Here are some common crate problems that can occur and how to deal with them:

Barking
Barking might occur when a dog is in desperate need of a bathroom break. While it is vital to pay attention to your dog's potty calls, it is also crucial to ignore cage barking when it is simply his plea to get out and play or snuggle. If he has been drinking or eating right before being put in the crate, he probably needs to go potty. If he does this as soon as he is put in his crate, and this behavior stops as soon as you give him attention, then this is his plea to get out of the crate. The more you let him out on command, the more the behavior is reinforced, and the harder it will be to teach him to keep quiet in his crate. If you are just starting your dog's crate training, make sure he has had a chance to empty his bowels and bladder so you know he will not have to go. Ignore his barking and release him from the crate when he is

calm. He may be silent for a few seconds at first. So, he knows it is the calm behavior that gets him out of the crate; you can acknowledge this behavior with a "Yes!". Gradually increase the amount of time he must stay quiet before letting him out. If your dog has already learned to demand independence by barking, repeat the process described above. However, because the habit has previously been reinforced, it will take longer to break it.

If you want your dog to practice more of the behavior that works, you must demonstrate it to him. I don't suggest giving your dog a treat or handing him his favorite toy every time they start to bark. This will communicate to the puppy that every time they bark, they will get a treat, reinforcing the wrong behavior. To avoid this, take your dog out for a good walk or run, tiring them out and giving them enough time to potty. Tiring your puppy can mean different things depending on their breed, their age, and how much energy they have. Once they are tired and have had their potty break, they are more likely to rest well in their crate without barking. There are various ways to interrupt your dog's barking behavior and to start off, you can use your voice. You must have the crate within your reach to be able to do this so if this behavior is more prominent at night, make sure you move the crate in your bedroom. You can start by interrupting their barking with a simple "hey." This will stop them from barking, and as soon as they stop, make sure you praise them. If your voice is not enough, you may consider keeping your crate close enough to your bed for you to be able to tap it. This is something they will not be expecting, and they may stop barking and move around to investigate the sound. If your sleeping arrangement does not allow your crate to be close enough to you to tap or to interrupt their barking by using your voice, then you can consider attaching a leash to the door. Simply ignoring their barking may, in most cases, not be enough of a message for your dog to understand what you are expecting out of them. For full control of your dog's barking when you are around, it is best to have a mobile crate to move around the house and keep it close to you when you are preparing meals, working from home, or simply watching TV. This is something you may need to consider if you thought of purchasing a wooden crate. You may need a smaller crate that is slightly easier to move around for trips to the vet or keep moving around the house.

Whining

It is important to distinguish between whether your dog is whining about being kept in or because he wants to go outside to potty. To avoid this dilemma, make sure you take them out for a potty break before placing them in the crate. Do not answer right away. Check to see whether he stops since this will tell whether he requires a go outside. If he persists, approach the crate, and reassure him in a friendly manner. Keep in mind that training takes incremental progress and may even backtrack at times. If whining is mostly done at night while they sleep in their crate, try keeping the crate in your bedroom where they can see and feel you. Attach a leash to the crate. This will work best if you have a wire crate. Keep the leash attached to your bedside table. When they whine, take the leash, and move it slightly, and it will create a clicking sound that will get your puppy's attention. This should stop their whining, and when they do stop, make sure you applaud them and acknowledge their good behavior. This method should also work for barking at night. To reduce distraction at night to the minimum, you may also cover the crate. Be sure to leave enough ventilation by placing a piece of wood or cardboard on top of the crate, so the sheet you are placing on top does not block the air going through and makes sure your dog does not reach out for it from the crate and chews on it. You can also leave the back of a wire crate against the wall open for better ventilation. Make sure that before going to sleep, you work out your puppy to the maximum. A puppy bursting with energy will less likely go to bed as you try to sleep and will whine about being locked in the crate. To avoid whining in the crate, make sure you take your puppy to the crate periodically during the day and not only when you are leaving the house. This will have them know that you will not be around and can end up throwing a tantrum to be let out. It is important to remember that whining is one of the few ways a puppy knows how to communicate, so it is best to not punish them for doing so. Even if you do, they are still too young to understand why they are being punished. The whining may be for several different reasons, including being scared, lonely, bored, uncomfortable, hurt, feeling sick, need to pee, hungry, or simply because they crave your attention. Whining is a natural thing dogs do to get attention, and if they have been recently brought home, they may do so to signal to their siblings that they are lost. Make sure you reassure them that you are close by, especially for the very first few days. Leave safe and fun toys in their crate to make sure they understand that their crate is safe enough to be in. Make sure you leave time for fun and interactive crate games. Whining can be used to signal that they are uncomfortable, maybe because their crate is too small or they are not comfortable, so make sure this is avoided before crating them. Drinking or eating close to the crating time may mean that their whining is because they need to go potty. This means that your dog is starting to be housetrained, but avoiding accidents in their crate, make sure food and drinks are stopped from one to a few hours before crating. Tired dogs or entertained dogs will more likely behave well in their crate. In some cases, your puppy may be hurt, and since their way of communicating with humans is limited, whining is one of the ways they express this. To make sure this is not the case, you can rub your puppy, touching all their joints. If they whine at any given time, then pain may be the reason for their continuous whining. Speak to your vet if this is the case. If you notice that your dog lacks energy, is not being so enthusiastic around you as before, has vomiting, diarrhea, or has not gone for some time, this may be a sign that they are sick. They may also be licking an area excessively, which could mean they have a skin infection or parasites. These could all be accompanied by excessive whining. Speak to your veterinarian if you notice such signs. If you think that your dog is whining because they do not have enough food, make sure you monitor their behavior in between meals. If they are full of energy in between meals, then this means you are feeding them well. It is best to ask your vet about the amount of food you should be feeding your dog. If they lack energy in between meals, it may also be because you are not feeding them their ideal portions. This depends on your dog's breed and age. From the age of eight to twelve months, dogs usually experience what is referred to as the bonding stage. Here, your dog will understand who its owners are and are able to establish a close bond. To avoid them whining because they crave your attention while crated, make sure you give them loads of love and attention whilst they are outside of the crate.

Crate or potty accidents
To avoid crate accidents, make sure the dog hasn't had anything to eat or drink for at least one hour before crating. Make sure the dog goes outdoors to relieve himself first. If he does his business in his crate even when he isn't over-crated, the first thing you should do is rule out medical issues. A dog's ability to hold it for typical periods of time is hampered by loose stools, a urinary tract infection, or other incontinence issues. Assuming everything is in order, there are a few probable reasons for crate soiling. Before, your dog may have been over-crated and forced to litter his crate, so his resistance to soiling his den has been weakened. He now considers soiling the crate is acceptable. Your dog isn't going outside to relieve himself before being crated. During his separation anxiety panic attack, your dog is voiding his bladder and bowels. The way you handle crate-soiling behavior is determined by the cause. If he is learned to litter his crate, changing his bedding, or removing it altogether until he is retrained may help. Your dog will be more comfortable in his soiled crate if you use absorbent bedding, such as a blanket. It is possible that his current bedding has evolved into his favorite habitat. Instead of bedding, try newspaper, a square of heavy-duty compressed foam rubber, or no bedding at all. A leash could be a good substitute for keeping your dog in the crate throughout the night. Maybe you are not checking to see if he has gone potty outdoors before putting him in his crate. You put him out in the backyard in the morning rush to get to work on time, assuming he will empty his bladder before returning inside. That could be a flawed belief. He might have huddled on the back porch, waiting to be invited back in, if it was chilly or raining. Perhaps he was preoccupied with looking for ants behind a shrub or barking at

the children passing by on their way to school. Perhaps he'll get a biscuit for returning home, so he'll avoid the step where he is meant to pee on the grass first. It could be a problem with habitat choice he wants to urinate on grass but can only find snow! Set an earlier alarm to allow you to walk him before and after he eats his meals to ensure he is not full when you crate him. Create a protected pee area if he is hesitant to go outside in bad weather, so he doesn't have to eliminate under pouring rain on his head or strong winds buzzing him. If he insists on going on grass when it is the dead of winter, you may have to brush snow off the grass in his covered pee spot or supply indoor-grown grass until you can teach him a new habitat preference.

Refusing to enter the crate

Crate-refusing dogs may have never been crate trained, or the crating process may have been mismanaged in some way. He may have been over-crated, and he now refuses to enter a crate where he fears being forced to the soil. Someone may have used his crate as a punishment or forcibly imprisoned him in a crate in the past. He could have had a negative experience in a crate that was incorrectly fastened and rolled with him in it, or he could have been put in a crate while loud noises or other fear-inducing stimuli were around. Whatever the motive, you will need to start a counterconditioning and exposure program to shift his negative associations to positive ones and retrain his crating behavior. Begin by putting tasty treats around the exterior of his crate, with a handful of nibbles placed just inside the entrance so he can reach them. To encourage him deeper in, gradually put additional yummies inside the crate. Start hand-feeding treats while he is inside when he is going in readily to encourage him to stay. Close the door slowly, feed treats through the door, and then let him out when he goes in and stays happily inside the crate while you feed treats. Increase the time you keep the door shut until he is completely comfortable with it. Return to give him his treat after taking a step away from the crate. Repeat until you notice that he is happy to remain in his crate. You can motivate him by playing different games. Put something delectable in the crate, such as a juicy knucklebone. Show it to your dog, then shut the door behind him while he is still outside the crate. If he wants to claim his prize, let him spend some time attempting to get into the closed crate to get to the bone, then open the door and let him zoom in and out. Make sure to play crating games with your dog on a regular basis, not just when he is about to be put in the crate for long periods of time. If your dog is adamant about going into the crate, get one that disassembles. Remove the top and begin the counter-conditioning procedure.

Panicking in the crate
This is not the same as demand barking. Some dogs, particularly those with SA, are unable to endure being confined in a crate. They have a full-fledged panic attack and try desperately to flee their cage. They may frantically attempt to bite and claw their way out, often breaking teeth and ripping out nails in the process. They can also have stress-induced urination and defecation, which they may proceed to paint all over the walls of their crate as they stomp around. You must address the SA problem through behavior change, and if you are successful in doing so, you may be able to crate train your dog in the future. Look into doggie day-care management options in the interim.

Aggressive behavior in the crate

The best response to this behavior is management, followed by behavior change. Dogs who are hostile in their crates should not be exposed to circumstances that continuously stimulate the behavior. At canine sporting events, for example, these dogs should not be left crated and unattended. If there are children around, they must not approach him in his crate. If the crate is covered, some dogs will go in calmly so reduce the stimuli that cause their hostility. Others perform fine if the crate contains nothing of high value, such as a beloved toy. If he is scared and retreating to his crate, make sure you do not intimidate him while he is in there—no reaching in to take bowls, toys, or the dog from the crate, for example. To avoid crate aggression, you should avoid putting a nervous dog in a crate until he has gained confidence in his relationship with you. If your dog is aggressive towards strangers, sit close to the crate with a huge supply of high-value treats. When your dog notices another human that triggers their aggression, start feeding him goodies nonstop until the person passes by. Wait for your dog to notice the signal each time it appears. Then, once the trigger is gone, keep giving him little portions of treat nonstop. Monitor your dog's reaction. You are searching for a shift in his reaction to the trigger's appearance, from wary to relaxed. When you regularly obtain the latter reaction, move the trigger closer to the crate and repeat the lessons until the trigger can pass right next to it. Suppose your approach causes your dog to become aggressive; practice walking up to the crate and dropping chicken into it so that your dog learns to identify your approach with nice things. Never punish your dog for being hostile in his crate; you will only make the problem worse!

Chewing anything in the crate
He is probably teething and wants to chew on anything to relieve the pain in his gums and jaws. He could also be bored out of his mind. So, start by removing all his bedding from his crate. You can give him an old towel when he is done teething if he doesn't require it right now. Before putting him in his crate, make sure he has had a good play session, a good walk, food, and a chance to relieve himself. Do not cut corners on any of these; if you are going to keep him confined, he needs to burn off some energy, spend time with you, eat and relieve himself.

When to stop crate training
Depending on the reason for crate usage, he may eventually stop needing one. This is especially true for pups who are crated when you need to be away from them, such as when you are at work or asleep or when they're learning to use the toilet outside. If you've kept your puppy in a crate for housetraining purposes, it is recommended that you establish a two-month deadline from the last indoor accident. That is, if your puppy hasn't soiled the insides of his crate or pottied in the house for two months, it is time to start looking into phasing out the crate. Furthermore, if your dog goes to his crate freely before bedtime or when he is clearly stressed out by the environment and needs a peaceful place to withdraw, you do not need to enforce crating as much. If he already uses it on his own, you can experiment with keeping it unlocked for periods of time so he can come and go as he pleases. If you are thinking of getting rid of a crate, take it slowly and cautiously. After all that training, you do not want to set your dog up to fail. You can begin by letting your puppy or dog out of the crate for longer periods of time between crate sessions. Always

give your dog a pee break before these out-of-crate adventures and try to avoid scheduling them shortly after a meal or a substantial drink of water. This extra time out of the crate will necessitate greater monitoring around the house at first, so do it when you have time to pay extra close attention to them. You will eventually be able to leave your dog out of the crate for longer, such as at night or while you are at work. Rather than giving them free access to the entire property, continue to restrict them but utilize a larger area than the crate, such as a pen, to set them up for success. Your dog may eventually progress to a larger area, such as the kitchen, before making all your shared space available. While you are gone, keep your dog occupied with a favorite toy or a frozen treat that takes a long time to eat. This will help them focus on one thing, preventing destruction and possible relapses in bathroom-break habits. You may notice that they have stopped chewing on things, are no longer anxious when you are out of their sight, and can pee where appropriate after holding it for a while. These are indicators that your dog may be let out of the crate for longer and more often. This does not mean that you will discard your crate for good. You may still use it for traveling, for trips to the vet, or when taking your dog to new and unfamiliar places.

Chapter 9:
Ameliorating Separation Anxiety with Crate training

For dogs with separation anxiety (SA), crate training can be quite useful, although it may not be the sole solution. Having a safe location where they can relax and unwind while alone is not only beneficial during separation anxiety therapy, but it also stops them from indulging in damaging conduct around the house.

There are two types of separation anxiety: genuine separation anxiety and simulated separation anxiety, in which the dog's behavior looks to be separation anxiety but is a taught behavior. When a dog lacks leadership and self-control, it typically exhibits simulated separation anxiety. True separation anxiety causes the dog to be extremely stressed when its owner is not there. In simulated separation anxiety, the dog is aware that if he misbehaves, he will receive attention. Even being verbally punished for such behavior can be pleasant for some dogs because they feel acknowledged. In many circumstances, negative attention can be a reward if the owner is uninformed that his dog's needs are not being met. There is little genuine tension in these situations, only misbehavior. Simulated separation anxiety is relatively easy to eliminate with a steady strategy that gradually increases the amount of time spent in a crate at home and away, consistent obedience training, adequate exercise, and good leadership. Dog owners frequently unintentionally encourage separation anxiety in their dogs. When you leave or return home, you make a great deal out of it, which reinforces the dog's anxiety about your absence and causes him to become even more stressed. You enjoy having your dog with you, and you take them everywhere. Then you must leave them alone, but they have grown with the need to be with you. You are their friend, their protector, and their family. Dog separation anxiety can be triggered by a change in habit, but boredom and lack of exercise can also lead to destructive behavior and stress.

If your dog suffers from separation anxiety, you should take your time introducing them to their crate. Patience is crucial when it comes to forming a favorable association with being crated. Not only when you are leaving, but also when you are still at home, practice leaving them in their crate. If your dog develops the habit of only going into their crate when you leave, the crate will become yet another source of stress for them. Allow them to spend time in their crate while you eat meals, rest in the same room, or work in your office down the hall. Begin with short periods of time and gradually increase the amount of time he spends in it. Allow him to have his favorite bone to use as a stress reliever while he is there. Look for strategies to control his barking in the crate. Teaching him to be calm is beneficial, as is interrupting his barking, so he learns there is no reward for it. In extreme circumstances, a barking collar may be used to keep your dog from barking while you are away. Nobody wants irritated neighbors, and this device will correct him while you are away. A comfortable sleeping area or an open crate, water, and a few safe, interactive puzzle toys should all be included in an extended confinement setting. Calming dog scents can be lightly sprayed on their crate bedding or diffused in a nearby diffuser for dogs with separation anxiety. Calming music or white noise can help some dogs with separation anxiety, especially when they are crated.

Stay near the crate while training your dog to stay inside, so he doesn't have separation anxiety attacks. Place the crate in a high-traffic area such as the living room, den, or bedroom, so he is not alone. Assure him that this is a secure location by speaking in a friendly tone. Use food and treats to entice him inside. Fill the crate with a blanket or towel, as well as chew toys, to show that it is a welcoming environment. Do not push him to enter. To be successful, crate training must be a pleasurable experience. Try to leave the room for short amounts of time and then return. As you depart, your dog may look up from his treats, but he should not be alarmed. You might merely leave for five to ten seconds at first, then return after walking up and down the corridor. Make sure your dog does not become agitated. You want him to know that you will come back even if you leave. You may increase the amount of time you leave your dog alone. In one week, you will not be able to move from ten seconds to three hours. Their learning depends on their patience. In his crate, your dog should have hundreds of happy memories. You should assure that he has something to chew on every time he enters his crate, and you return everything he sees you leave.

Separation anxiety cannot be solved with just a crate. You cannot just shove a dog with severe separation anxiety and hope for the best. However, if you combine crate training with a lot of good interactions and progressively increase the time you leave your dog alone, it can be a useful tool. Crates efficiently stop some dogs with separation anxiety from moving excessively. Teach your dog to tolerate the crate. Allow him to explore under supervision, learning the limits and restrictions of his surroundings and developing respect for it and the people who live in it. That involves being consistent in everything you do with your dog, including everyone in your family who interacts with him.

Chapter 10:
Mistakes to avoid when crate training

If you do not know where to start or how to do it successfully, you will be frustrated, and your dog will suffer as well. If you wish to start crate training a dog for his safety and comfort, make sure you avoid these frequent blunders:

1. Hiding the crate

Many owners dislike the appearance of their dog's crate and hide it in an unused room. This is a tremendous blunder. Your dog may not wish to use the dog crate if it is placed in a room where no one spends any time. The dog may feel lonely. When crate training your dog, keep it in the room where you spend the most time, such as the living room. Your dog will be more comfortable in his crate since he is aware that you are still around. You can cover the crate with cardboard or wood boards if you do not like the way it looks. Your dog will not mind; many dogs prefer their crates to be dark and cool. Decorate it to complement the rest of your home's furnishings.

2. Stripping the crate to its bare minimum

It will be uncomfortable and unwelcoming for your dog if you leave it vacant. Put a cozy dog bed inside or anything else that makes it feel more like home to the dog, and transform it into a nice little sanctuary. When choosing one, think about your dog's preferences. If he enjoys soft and fluffy pet beds, get him one. A cooler dog bed, a thin bed, or even simply a blanket may be preferred by a larger dog. To keep your dog entertained, throw some toys or chews in his crate. Soft dog toys that he would enjoy cuddling with and firm chews are both good options. Make sure these are tough objects that will not choke him if they're ripped apart. When crate training dogs, putting items inside will help keep your dog occupied. It will also demonstrate to him that his crate is a secure location containing all his favorite items.

3. Rushing the process

Many owners make the mistake of simply locking their dog in the crate and walking away for hours at a time. This can make your dog fear the crate, which can lead to serious crate training and housebreaking concerns down the road. To get the greatest results, progressively introduce your dog to his crate when you initially get it. Begin by allowing your dog to explore his crate at his leisure. He'll probably sniff about and wander in and out to see what's going on. Some dogs take to their crate immediately; if yours does, that is fantastic! If that doesn't work, start praising the dog for going into the crate on his own; praise and treats are great options. You should also try fun games with your dog that involves the crate, which I've discussed extensively in a previous chapter. Before you put him in, don't forget to make sure he doesn't need to go potty.

4. Using the crate as a punishment

Never use your dog's crate as a punishment if you want him to see it as his safe place. Associating the crate with punishment will make your dog fear it and stop going into his crate willingly. Dogs, in general, respond better to positive treatment. Positive praise, treats, and playtime is all effective methods for teaching your dog proper behavior. The only time you should use your crate as a form of punishment is if your dog is too enthusiastic. If he needs to calm down, telling him to go into his crate will allow him to do so. He should still be rewarded after doing so.

5. Using commands in a conflicting manner

Decide on one word to use as a command for going inside the crate when crate training dogs. When instructing him, keep this one word in mind. If you use other commands, your dog will become confused and frustrated. This may cause problems with crate training, and he may refuse to obey you. Keep in mind that hand signals are also crucial. Many dogs are more responsive to hand gestures than to spoken commands. Try pointing towards your dog's crate to get him into it. Allow him to become accustomed to this signal and refrain from using that hand motion for any other commands. This ensures that your instruction is apparent to your dog and that he understands what you are asking of him.

6. Buying a crate that is too small or too big for your dog

Before buying a crate, make sure you measure your dog and buy one that will serve the purpose you intend it for. Having a crate that is too big may have your dog litter on one side while they sleep on the other side. A crate that is too small may have him become frustrated inside it and have physical and health repercussions.

7. Over-crating

Although crating can be the solution for your puppy's housebreaking patterns and provide you with the peace of mind that he is safe at home while you are at work, the crate is not a storage box. Even an adult dog cannot be locked up for 10 hours at a time. Puppies will need to have someone take them out for potty breaks, feed, and play with them halfway through the morning and the afternoon, so make arrangements for this. Avoid leaving your dog crated for a long time, especially if he is still a puppy. This may force them to pee in the crate and remain in their mess until you return from work. Over-crated dogs do not get enough exercise or human connection and will become unhappy or nervous. To lessen the amount of time your dog spends in its crate each day, you may need to adapt your schedule, hire a pet sitter, or enroll your dog in a day-care facility. Puppies under six months are not meant to be kept in a crate for more than three to four hours at a time. They cannot keep their bladders or bowels under control for that much time. Adult dogs that have been housetrained have the same limitations. Your dog's home may be a crate, but just as you wouldn't spend your entire life in one room of your house, your dog should not spend most of his time in his crate.

8. Leaving your dog with a collar in the crate

When a dog is in the crate, no collars, tags, or other items should be worn. The dog could strangle themselves if the tag gets trapped in the crate. Make sure they are left naked when crated.

9. **Let children tease your dog while he is crated.**

You want to establish positive notions between your dog and his crate, and the last thing you want is for him to think that outside the crate is where he should be.

10. **Leaving him to play with dangerous toys unsupervised in the crate.**

Make sure that the toys you leave him with when he is on his own are not toys he can potentially choke on.

11. **Not allowing enough time for your dog to pee before crating him.**

Potty breaks a huge part of crate training. If he is not let out frequently and for enough time to go potty, he may have accidents in the crate.

12. **Crating your puppy without enough playtime**

Dogs require frequent walks and exercise, which varies according to their breed, as some need more exercise time than others. It is important to let your dog burn off some energy before putting them in their crates. They will end up frustrated and anxious if this is not done. The crate is comfortable for them, but it is ultimately a restricted place, so chewing toys will not help them to burn energy. Besides, playtime will ensure your dog uses his crate time to unwind and relax, making them enjoy their time in there and guaranteeing quiet time for you too.

13. Letting your puppy out when he whines or barks.

If you let your dog out of the crate when he is whining, you communicate to him that making noise gets him out. Before letting him out, wait for silence or at least a respite in the whining. However, determining whether he is whining because he needs to defecate can be difficult at times. At first, try to ignore the whining. If your dog is putting you to the test, he should stop in a reasonable amount of time. He may need to go potty if he continues to whine for more than a few minutes. Wait for a pause in the whining, then release him and immediately take him outdoors to pee.

14. Punish your dog when he is in the crate.

While your dog is in his crate, don't scold or penalize him. Keep his crate experiences enjoyable by praising him, feeding him treats, or giving him more attention than usual while he is in there.

15. Putting newspaper of house-training pads IN the crate.

Newspaper or housetraining pads should not be placed in the crate. These items can stimulate your dog to go potty, which is exactly what you don't want him to do while confined. Because your dog will instinctively not want to pollute the space where he sleeps, the crate is designed to take advantage of his natural instinct to hold it.

16. **Making a big deal when leaving or returning home.**

Make no hassle about your departures and arrivals. Before leaving for work, put your dog in its crate and ignore it for twenty minutes. When you get home, take him out of the crate and outside to go potty right away, but keep the greeting interaction with them low-key. It is suggested that you crate him for brief periods of time when you are at home, so he doesn't link crating with being alone.

17. **Sleep on the sofa because your dog will not stop crying when you leave them to go to bed, and their crate is located all the way in the living room.**

Dogs catch up quite fast, and if they notice that you give in when they cry or whine, they will continue with this behavior until you give up crate training altogether. Make sure you are consistent and persistent with this training and move the crate to the bedroom next to yours if this happened but avoid letting them out when they whine or bark unless they are about to have an accident.

Chapter 11:
TOP tips for crate training

When adding a dog to your family or household, crate training can be an advantageous management technique. When you know you cannot supervise or will not be at home as often as you wish to, crate training can assist in speeding up the housetraining process and prevent undesirable or negative behavior. In your automobile, a crate is also a safe option for carrying your pet.

Here are some of the TOP tips for crate training:

- Go for a wire crate with a pull-out tray from the bottom. They're easier to clean and provide your dog a better view of the world around him.

- Get a crate that is appropriate for your dog; it should allow him to sit or stand, move around, and lie down comfortably.

- If you are adopting a young puppy and buying a crate big enough so he can grow in it, you should obtain a partition panel. This means you may modify the size of the crate's inside room to fit your dog's needs as he matures.

- Place soft, washable bedding inside the crate to make it cozier and more welcoming.

- Put your dog's crate in the quietest area of one of the house's busiest rooms, like the family room, so that he does not link crating with being secluded or banished.

- Introduce the crate to your dog gradually. Do not rush the process.

- Feed meals in the crate, so your dog associates the crate with positive things.

- Do not increase the time they spend in the crate all at once, but gradually.

- Leave significant toys in the crate for your dog to play with and reinforce positive associations with the crate.

- If you start feeding your puppy meals in his crate, make sure you do not leave the food bowl full in the crate for longer than fifteen minutes.

- Only leave chew proof and soft toys in the crate when unsupervised.

- In his crate, place an old, unwashed t-shirt if your dog does not have a habit of chewing on things, especially if he is past the teething phase already. Your dog will be able to always scent you, which will provide him great comfort. It will give him the impression that you are always nearby.

- Only allow your puppy in the bed with you when they have progressed with their crate training, stopped chewing on almost everything within their reach, and stopped having accidents for a while.

- Do not choose a fluffy blanket, but a suitable dog pad or bed. It is understandable that you want to get your puppy a wonderfully soft fluffy blanket. While it may appear to be the proper thing to do, it really encourages him to shred it to pieces, which is a bad habit that needs to be broken.

- Use a puppy toy that is less than two months old. There are many different viewpoints on whether pups should have toys in their crates. It is essential to keep an eye on your puppy when he is playing with toys since you don't want him tearing chunks off and choking on them. However, your dog will be extremely stressed the first few nights he arrives. A soothing toy in his crate, especially when he gets home, could be beneficial. It is important to do this while he is still little and incapable of ripping anything. It is doubtful that your puppy's teeth or mouth will be strong enough to shred a toy before three months. This makes it ideal to use a snuggle puppy.

- Because food is one of your puppy's top interests, having him eat his meals inside the crate can quickly establish a positive link. Place the bowl right at the entrance of the crate, with the door open, if your dog is comfortable enough to go inside. Allow him to eat as he pleases but keep the bowl near the crate. Start putting his bowl inside as they get used to it, but don't shut the door! Keep the door open since you are not attempting to fool him.

- Be attentive to how your puppy interacts with his crate throughout the early stages of crate training. Encourage your puppy as he becomes accustomed to his crate and shows interest in it. Always give him lots of praise. Because you are creating good associations and encouraging rewarding behavior, positive reinforcement-based training works well. All puppies are likely to repeat something that gives them a good response from their owner.

- Using a blanket or covering the crate works well and gives his crate a more den-like appearance and feel. The key is to gradually introduce it to him. After your dog has become accustomed to his crate, try covering it with a blanket, but only covering the single top panel. This way, it won't be too dark or unusual. As your puppy grows, experiment with covering the sides as well to see how he reacts.

- It is understandable for your puppy to be uneasy in their crate at first, and this is mostly because they have been separated from their siblings or mother. You can use a heartbeat dog, which is essentially a soft toy with a vibration device inside to mimic the heartbeat of a dog. If your puppy is too small and may chew the toy, you can place it over the crate whilst it is covered at night. The vibrations can still get to the crate, and the puppy will feel relaxed at night, resulting in a good night's sleep for both of you.

Always monitor your puppy in the crate to get a sense of what they like and don't like, which will help you have a successful crate training experience.

Chapter 12:
Puppy Crate training Q&A's

If you have recently added a four-legged family member to your household, and this is your first time, you may feel lost.

These are some of the commonest questions and answers new puppy owners ask:

1. Where can I find a crate?

They are available at hardware and retail stores. A pet supply company may be your best bet for the widest assortment and, sometimes, the best bargain. Crates come in a variety of forms and materials, with some being more durable or practical than others. Follow my advice on the different types of crates and how to choose the best one.

2. How will a crate stop my dog from chewing everything within their reach?

When you cannot be there to oversee an untrained puppy, you should crate him to prevent accidents. The same goes for a dog who chews or gets into mischief when you cannot be present to supervise him. When confined to a crate, a destructive dog can only chew on the toys you give him, not your furniture or pillows!

3. Can I crate train an older dog?

Puppies learn at a faster rate than older canines. Allow him to sniff and inspect the crate with the door open at first. Allow him to eat his food in it and jump in and out for goodies. Make the crate a comfortable place to stay, just like you would with a puppy, and keep crating periods short at first. Many dogs, once acclimated to them, like spending time in crates even when they are not required to. Crates are a popular spot to hide with a new toy or get away from a rowdy puppy or children. There may be several crates around the house, and dogs can be found snoozing in them with the doors wide open at any time. They may even fight over who gets to use it if you have multiple dogs.

4. **Can a dog become afraid of the crate instead of falling in love with it during the training phase?**

When utilized correctly, a crate or dog cage can be an excellent training tool. When used incorrectly or excessively, it can be a source of terror and torment. A crate should be used by every dog, especially new puppies. Dogs are descended from wild canines who sought cover in dens. The den, a compact, snug, and safe shelter for sleeping and rearing puppies, is dug by most wild canines. Domesticated dogs instinctively want such a haven. Keeping your dog for eight hours, overnight, or while you are at work is not animal cruelty, especially if the dog has been taken for a long walk or run before being crated. People who crate their dogs for extended periods of time should consider why they wanted a dog in the first place. It is customary to send a child to his room as a kind of punishment. Dogs are not children in coats, and using this strategy to teach them a lesson is ineffective. When it comes to correcting a dog's negative behavior, it is critical to catch him in the act. Dogs are completely focused on the present and do not associate what they did five minutes or a half-hour ago with the present. Frequently, an owner discovers the mess and punishes the dog without knowing whether the 'sin' occurred five minutes, a half-hour, or more recently. "I obeyed when they called, I got punished for it, and I surely won't make the mistake of coming when called again"— this is what the dog associates with being called over, punished, and then thrown in a crate. He then thinks the crate is a bad and frightening environment. This approach will surely scare the dog from the crate.

5. What are all the confinement options for my dog?

It may be easy to dog-proof your home or apartment by closing a few doors or installing child gates or barricades, depending on your situation. The dog may then be given access to the rest of the house. Another alternative is to employ avoidance devices, such as motion detectors and citronella spray collars, to keep your pet away from certain places. If you must go without this dog-proofing, restrict the dog to a single room, pen, or crate. The smaller confined area ensures your dog's protection while also protecting your property from harm. It teaches your dog what is and is not permitted to chew or go potty in that particular location.

6. Is crate training suitable for ALL dogs?

Crate training may cause anxiety in some dogs, and they may continue to go potty while confined. Different sorts of confinement, such as pens, limited rooms, or walled places, frequently suit these dogs better. When placed in the crate, continued uneasiness, damage, or emotional distress may indicate separation anxiety. In these situations, a behavior intervention may be required.

7. Will crate training induce barking?

A crate is a common tool for reducing or preventing distress barking. Instead of keeping a puppy locked away from its owners at night or during meals, the puppy could be kept in a crate in the bedroom or kitchen. If the owners are in the same room, the puppy cannot get into mischief and is less likely to bark. Distress vocalization is considerably more likely if the puppy is confined to an area with no access to its humans. If the owner approaches the puppy to calm it down or check on it, the puppy interprets this as a reward for its barking.

Conclusion

Crate training a dog can take a few days or weeks, depending on the temperament, age, and prior crate experience of the dog. The key to good training is to make it enjoyable and take it in little, methodical steps.

You should be prepared to train for anywhere from three days to six months. Because dogs aren't linear learners, there may be ups and downs, but success will come. Even if you feel hopeless at times, if you keep calm and persistent in your approach, your dog can ultimately obey, and you will be able to reward them.

I trust this book has provided you with all the information you need to successfully crate train your dog. From a dog crate training schedule to choosing a crate to where to put it, this book covered it all. The advantages of giving your dog his own tiny home or safe zone are significant.

After a puppy arrives in its new home, it is worth the time and effort to acclimate it to its crate. Crate training issues should be addressed early in the process, properly considered, and worked out. Forcing the issue is never a good idea because it can only make things worse. Patience and understanding of the puppy's concerns are essential. There are four things a new puppy owner should make sure their future dog has to keep it healthy for the rest of its life. The first is good veterinary care, the second is training and limit settings, the third is neutering non-breeding dogs, and the fourth is constant access to a crate. Your motto, as a dog owner, should be "a crate for life."

www.ingramcontent.com/pod-product-compliance
Lightning Source LLC
Chambersburg PA
CBHW070316120526
44590CB00017B/2696